T0103866

THE
CHRONICLE
OF MY
STRUGGLE

drgokulan

PARTRIDGE
A Penguin Random House Company

To order additional copies of this book, contact
Toll Free 800 101 2657 (Singapore)
Toll Free 1 800 81 7340 (Malaysia)
orders.singapore@partridgepublishing.com

www.partridgepublishing.com/singapore

To my wife Mrs Jayasree Madakkavil, without whom, in all likelihood I would not have been where I am now and to my twin children Jayaram and Sriram. I am proud of them.

ACKNOWLEDGMENTS

The chronicle of my struggle is the sum total of the experiences I had in Malaysia and in the UK in the late nineteen nineties. It was my friend and renowned Malayalam Novelist Mr Sreekumar E P who found sparks in my jottings of these experiences and has since given me lots of encouragement to introduce it to the readers of the current frame. I am truly grateful to him.

My most sincere thanks

- to Mr Harisankar A V of the Malayalamanorama, the famous Malayalam daily of Kerala state in India who helped me do the greater part of editing out of his busy official commitments.
- to Prof. Dominic K V, a retired professor of English at Newman College in Thodupuzha of Kerala, for his valuable corrections and the suggestion for the title of this book.
- to Mr Balakrishnan Ulliyeri the Artist of Mathrubhumi, a National daily in Malayalam, for the cover design.
- to Mr Madanamohanan P V, popularly known as Madanan, the Art Editor of Mathrubhumi, for his

magnificent touch in making the interior illustrations interesting.

- to Mr Madhavkumar B and Mrs Gina Biju Justus for their sincere effort in the final amendments in the editing part of this book.
- to Dr M Muraleedharan of Sree Krishna College of Guruvayoor in Kerala.
- to all my friends and well-wishers.

Our greatest weakness lies in giving up. The most certain way to succeed is always to try just one more time.

Thomas A. Edison

Contents

CHAPTER ONE

A flash back

I do not know where to start from, perhaps a long way back, right from the beginning. My early days often whizzes past me as I watch my children progress through the different phases of life.

I was the third among the six children of my parents.

Nettur, the place I spent my childhood was not aware of the outer cosmos. It was a village in every sense of the 'word' as hardly was there any modern convenience to speak of.

As for my schooling, I went to a local school nearby for my lower elementary grades. It was just a doorstep close. Infact I don't remember my mom either accompanying me to school or waiting to fetch me after school hours like many of the other kids.

I did not carry a school bag or a water bottle nor were we given any school uniform. As I fondly remember those were the days of hesitancy, and apprehension. Very often I would find myself hiding under the wooden table as the forenoon bell rang!

I attended my higher secondary a little farther off from home. I had to walk quite a stretch and even use a ferry too, to reach school! Often it felt as though school was even farther off than usual. I was not a bright student those days; moreover I was an easy prey for sickness. All this made me feel a little isolated.

Jose Tom was a studious boy. So were Paulose P X, Augustine J Puthussery and Abraham Varghese. My teachers often liked them. I remember feeling shrunken and neglected as I thought over this. Nevertheless I used to look at them with admiration. If only I could be like them, I would be liked as well!

My extremely poor math skill made life in school miserable. Every day I woke up early in the morning for my Mathematics tuition. Everyone would be fast asleep and most of the time I would find myself attending classes on an empty stomach, although sometimes mom would get me some black tea.

I used to cluster my books with the help of a black rubber band. To walk with my fastened books in one hand and the umbrella in the other was no small task, especially when it rained.

Sometimes we would be in the middle of the river when a downpour would start. There were no motor boats. The boatman dipped the long bamboo pole under water to give the boat a forward thrust. The boat would always be crowded. We used to sit on the boat's rim which very often touched the water line. We would dip our fingers in the water to enjoy the turbulence it created. Every time the boatman's long bamboo pole touched the water, I would watch in fascination the ripples on the surface which expanded concentrically and finally disappeared. We were least bothered, slightly cared to understood how risky this travel was, especially when it rained and so did our parents, unless some mishap occurred. So audacious were those days.

I was shorter than most of my peers in class and so it happened that I appeared weird to everyone around me. Many, including my mom, never expected I would as tall as I am today.

On the way to school I always passed by the tea shop of my neighborhood. It had a long table and a bench along the verandah that looked similar to the one, we as children had in our lower elementary school. The table always seemed dark and muddy, littered with left over crumbs and smears. Customers sat on the bench chattering to each other about the current affairs in the newspaper, which I could not fathom much. I used to watch the tea vendor making tea much to my curiosity. He was a tall man whose skinny stature was marked with a distinctive crook on the back. He wore a dhoti (a traditional menswear which is a plain cloth, 2 meters long and 1.25 meters wide, open at both ends) tightly around the waist, which always looked messy far below his navel. The other end of it was loosely folded above the knee level disclosing his bony legs. During his routines he always tried to fold it whenever it unfolded spontaneously. That taut face with the rapid motion of lips gave away the impression that he was muttering something in resentment.

He had two cans, one conical and the other cylindrical, both flat-bottomed and open at the other end. The metal handles of the cans were wrapped in cloth that always looked dark and filthy. With a tilt of his trunk towards left he lifted the can in his right hand high above his head and poured the hot tea into the lower one held in his left hand below, by the knee. Down came the tea cascading into the bottom can with splashes and roars. He repeated this gesture a couple of times and finally poured the tea into a small, stained glass tumbler till it foamed at the brim and overflowed.

I could see people reading the newspaper and enjoying steam cakes made of rice flour with meat curry. The smell that emanated from his shop tickled my nose. I used to hold my breath as I walked past the shop and my stomach growled in response. I had a ferocious appetite those days and always dreamt of eating lots of these dishes when I grew up and started earning!

I did not enjoy school at all. All sorts of complexes, from inferiority to insecurity enveloped me all the time. I found it difficult to cope with the change from the village school to the upper primary school in a bigger town. So far I had my studies in the local language and the sudden change to English medium made things worse.

My father was keen that I should excel in studies and he used to help me a lot. He had great ambitions for me and would sit down to teach me, on returning from office work. Looking back, I felt a huge block of darkness standing between me and the school environment.

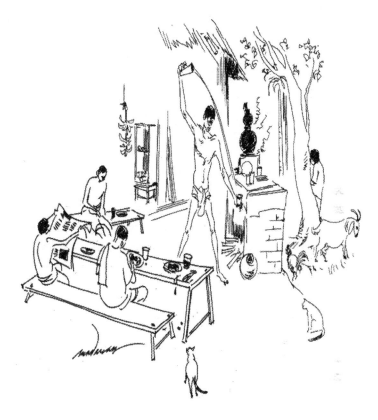

S T Jacob Sir taught us mathematics in standard V (first year of upper primary level). He was so furious over my Mathematics that he used to beat me with a cane till I started to bleed. I have shown these scars on my left leg to my children. Corporal punishment was much a common matter those days. Mathematics continued to be tough in high school as well and quite frankly, I was not a stranger to zero marks! In Standard VIII (first year of secondary level) at Sacred Heart High School of Thevara in Ernakulam (a district of Kerala state in India), Kartha Sir was the first teacher to award me a naught in Mathematics! My rank was ridiculously low in the class most of the time.

Like a small seed with hidden potential something was still driving me forward, but I couldn't figure what!

The turning point came when I met T P Swamy Sir while I was in Class IX (pre final year of secondary school level). It was my classmate George Joseph who introduced me to him for a private Mathematics tuition. Swami Sir was a Tamil Brahmin (upper class in Hindu religion) and by profession, he was not a school teacher per say. He was struggling to make both ends meet, so he gave part time tuitions even while working at the Coconut Development office in Ernakulam.

This was a huge changeover. I started to feel upraised from a world haunted by emotional repression into a state of optimism. I saw a bright ray of light, guiding me to wriggle myself out of a tunnel of intense darkness, leading me to the dazzling sun!

It really was a surreal experience. For the first time, I scored 61 marks out of 100 in Mathematics! I simply could not believe that arduous ascent.

Many teachers have taught me in different stages of my education. Yet to none of them have I owed as much as I did to Swami Sir. He was a great soul who revitalized my resolve. Even though I do not know his whereabouts, but still today I remember him with a sense of intense gratitude and teary eyes. Swami Sir had a son named Senthil, who had a younger and an elder sister. The elder sister was slightly darker in complexion like her mom but the younger one used to be a little chubby and fair.

I used to get a piping hot coffee every morning at his house during the class. I remember eagerly waiting for his wife to walk in with the coffee. It's unique aroma is still stays fresh in my mind. The coffee was infact a special privilege, as I was the only student in the morning session of the tuition class.

However, Swami Sir was not there to help me all the way to the end of my final year of the secondary school. He was transferred to Patna in Bihar (north-eastern state in India). I received a letter from him once and haven't heard from him since. Yet I will always cherish remembering the moments I had with him.

I took Biology stream at my Pre-University level. To see me don a doctor's coat was my father's dream. Later on, it became my ambition as well. Yet I never dared to speak about this secret wish as I believed it was something far beyond my caliber. I did my Bachelor's degree in Science (BSc) with Chemistry as my primary field of study. There too, I had to confront the specter of Mathematics as a subsidiary subject. However at the Pre-University level, being in the biology stream, Mathematics wasn't required at all. From the zeroes in Standard VIII to a cent percent at the BSc level was perhaps only because of Almighty's blessing, my unceasing self-motivation and hard work. Subsequently I got an admission-on-merit at the College of Engineering, Trivandrum, (capital of Kerala state) for the Electronics and Telecommunication branch. I spent six months at the College of Engineering only to hit a switch to Medicine.

Once I happened to meet Panicker Sir, my old Malayalam teacher in Standard X (final year of the secondary school level). He could not believe that I was a medical student. Skillfully concealing the astonishment that cropped up on his face, he was keen to know how I made it to the coveted Medical Colleges, where only the best got through. He was probing to get the result he was looking for and I could sense the hidden malice. I merely smiled and assured him in all respects that my admission to Medicine was purely based on merit.

Many of my school teachers and even my classmates could not endure this transition from a dull witted to a meritorious student. I cannot blame them too.

This is what I could recall from a stroll down my memory lane. I simply can't tell more about how the canvas of my childhood or adolescence looked like. These were just scratches from an illustrious past. That was all me.

CHAPTER TWO

Turning point

I was carrying on my journey, my mind full of ambitions. After getting a basic degree in Medicine (MBBS) and then a diploma in Child Health (DCh), I started practicing as a Child Specialist in 1992 at Tirur, a small town in the Malappuram district of Kerala state in India. The practice definitely brought in money, but life in Tirur did not give me much satisfaction. A feeling of incompleteness was casting shadows on my mind. One day after work, I sat down by my work desk, took out a piece of paper and jotted down, 'Dr Gokulan BSc, MBBS, DCh, MRCP (UK)'. The last degree title was a burning desire that I had craved for ever since I landed on a job. MRCP initialized for Member of the Royal College of Physicians is a postgraduate qualification in the United Kingdom and is the bull's eye for any doctor aspiring for a higher specialty in their medical career. And so I started dreaming about its possibility. Never did I expect it to actually happen. Yet I dreamt on just as a boy would fantasize an expensive toy! I never disclosed my thoughts to anybody. When I had discussed this with one of the professors of my undergraduate studies, all I got was discouragement. I kept that bit of paper for many days, hidden between the folios of my desires like a peacock feather in order to skim through it at times and enrich my mind with energy and verve.

As a matter of fact, there wasn't any inspiration from outside, yet it bred within me. To amass a fortune was the sole aim of many around me and I found it difficult to synchronize with them.

I took a decision to leave Tirur finally and went for a job in the Malaysian Ministry of Health as a contract medical officer. It was for a salary much less than what I used to earn from my private practice in Tirur.

I was practically alone when it came to making decisions. Nobody would hold my plans which seemed outlandish. I had no relatives or friends then in the UK. Moreover, how was I going to support myself there?

Financial limitations were then a stumbling block. So, going directly to the UK for the MRCP examination was beyond my dreams and I decided to move forward at a slower pace. Accepting a job in Malaysia had a twofold advantage; I could support my family and at the same time pursue my studies for the MRCP examination for which Malaysia was a center.

CHAPTER THREE

Malaysia

My memories of Malaysia are a downer with more of tears than happiness. It was a period of turmoil and intense hardships. My salary as a contract medical officer was hardly enough to support the family. During the weekends I used to work as a locum. This was an alternative to earn some quick needed cash. During the free hours of the week, doctors would work for other institutions. Sometimes I had to travel long distances and used to work continuously for 24-48 hours. Working as a locum was forbidden for ministry of health doctors, however many of them used to do it despite the risk.

My children were coerced to join an expensive International School, as the other schools did not propose an English curriculum. Education at an International school was very expensive and only the affluent could afford it, however I did not have any choice. The struggle to meet the family expenses was worsened by the tight and tiresome hospital schedules.

Being an expatriate school, the student community was multiracial and my children for the first time at that tender age tasted the bitterness of discrimination along with me. However,

I cannot forget the support and encouragement I received from a few consultants of Indian origin in my department and this kept me in good spirits.

I was supposed to reach the hospital by 7:00 AM and relentless hours of exhaustive work followed. I used to wake up at 3, early in the morning. It would be raining outside and most often my family would be fast asleep. I would take a quick shower, pray for a while and start preparing for the Part I of the MRCP examination till 7:00 AM. These four hours in the morning were all the time I could snatch out of the day for my studies without any interruption. It became part of my daily routine. Part I of the MRCP examination was a cakewalk for me. My self-esteem and confidence rose like a phoenix bird out of the ashes. Part II of the exam, the final, was performance based and I really had a tough time here. The expenses involved in appearing for the exam in Malaysia itself had cost me an arm and a leg considering my limited earnings!

After unsuccessful attempts, I was exhausted physically and financially but not mentally. Even then, there were many factors beyond my regulation that made it impossible for me to continue my stay in Malaysia. So after five years of feverish work, I came back home almost empty-handed with neither a degree nor any earnings. But the silver lining was the improvement in my academic skills which helped me lay down a strong foundation to build up my professional career.

CHAPTER FOUR

KEM Mumbai

My long cherished ambition remained, which often made me an object of ridicule especially before my in-laws. A feeling of isolation enveloped me.

What could I do next?

The main hurdle in going to the UK for the examination was of course, the financial capability. I had a small sum of money in hand, which I had saved as a locum in Malaysia. But this was definitely not enough to take me to the UK. All my efforts to make money were in vain. Darkness encircled me once again and I was desperately looking for the guiding light that could direct me. The only support I received was the motivation from my wife. She was keen that I should appear for the exam in the UK at any cost and even suggested how to acquire the means to go forward. The loan amount she managed to get from a local bank by pledging her gold ornaments was barely enough to meet the expenditure. So unconditional was the support from her part which I'd always carry in my heart with gratitude. That solved one problem. Ultimately my decision to go to the UK got consolidated. Only my wife and our children knew about this. The decision was precarious and ridden with risks. All the while it did feel as though I was balancing myself on a tightrope with a pole like a circus artist.

It had been four months since my return from Malaysia. The next examination in the UK is after 4 months. I had not opened my books at all ever since my arrival from Malaysia. I was starting to lose my touch with the subjects. I had to pull myself together, so I decided to join a good institution to have a final and thorough preparation. I made arrangements with the KEM (King Edward Memorial) Hospital in Mumbai city of Maharashtra state in India for a clinical attachment. A clinical attachment gave me access to both the clinical and academic routines of the department. This would give me the perfect environment for an effective preparation for the examination. The only downside was the lack of payment.

I was on my quondam journey once again. Only my family knew of my exact destination. As for everyone else, the word was that I was going to Malaysia again for a job assignment as I had instructed my wife to say so to anyone who asked her.

I was already tagged as an irresponsible bum who cared little for the family. To add to that, I was past my early forties, an age not considered suitable for taking such gambles. I was indeed confident of what I could achieve, but how could I convince the others? So I did not feel comfortable to share my ambition or anything that went on my mind with the others.

KEM Mumbai did not suit me well. Food became an issue. So did my intense feelings of nostalgia. The air around me was making me nervous and I did not carry out the program as I had planned. I left the KEM campus bidding none adieu. I felt relaxed temporarily, but was unsure of what to do next and where to go. I took my entire luggage and headed for the Mumbai Victoria Terminus (VT) railway station in a taxi. I did not have any reservation on any train bound for any destination and felt totally disoriented.

What could I do in the busiest station of this huge metro?

As I sat idle in the station, an Idea struck me. I managed to get a sleeper class reservation ticket through an agent to Katpady in Tamil Nadu state of India which could took me to the Christian Medical College (CMC), Vellore.

CHAPTER FIVE

CMC Vellore

I resumed the clinical attachment program, in the Pediatric Department of CMC Vellore. A priest of the CSI Church whom I met there offered me a rented accommodation in their guest house for a reasonable price.

The atmosphere at the CMC Vellore made me feel much better and life was generally smooth, barring some of the pangs of humiliation from certain department heads. The Royal College, the authority conducting the examination required that the application form for the MRCP examination should be supported by a senior doctor with higher levels of membership like FRCP (shortened for Fellow of Royal College of Physicians) or those who have MRCP with a minimum of 8 years of experience from the same royal college. The Pediatric Head of CMC was a Fellow of the same Royal College but to my surprise he refused to confirm my application by putting up some lame and silly excuses. What hurt me more than his fabrications were his attitude and body language. By then I had been attached to the department for a few months and I couldn't figure out a reason for his behavior. It almost broke my heart. A sudden hiatus in the momentum I had attained so far was well enough to tip me off my balance briefly. Yet, adversities were not new to me and I had already made up my mind to face anything on my way.

Meanwhile, I had got the UK visa stamped quite easily, requiring only an examination hall ticket and a proof of identity. The last date for the submission of the application was just around the corner and yet I had not found anyone to vouch for my application to take the examination. Without fulfilling this formality my application could even get rejected. I did have an extra application form which was attested by my previous department head in Malaysia. Though he knew me very well, I was not currently working under him. So technically, I would have to obtain prior approval from him to proceed with that application. My efforts to contact him in Malaysia went in vain. I had little choice now as the last date was closing in and my present department head (CMC) had rejected my pleas. With my fingers crossed, I sent the application that was supported by my previous department head in Malaysia.

I left CMC exactly twenty days prior to the theory examination in the UK and I had no idea where to stay in that strange country before the examination. So I decided to stay on in Chennai (the capital of Tamil Nadu state, India) for a while, waiting for something to work out. I had no means for a hotel stay in London for twenty days, no matter what class it belonged to. So I joined the Pediatric Cardiology department of the Madras Medical Mission, Chennai for another two weeks of clinical attachment. The idea was to shorten the costly days I would have to spend in the UK prior to my examination. I made some contacts with an India based social organization in the UK through emails. They had sound roots in Kerala and one person offered me a room for a rent of 50 pounds a week.

The clinical attachment at the Madras Medical Mission ended on time and the air ticket to the UK was arranged through a local travelling agency. I did some very essential shopping which included buying a pair of trousers and shirts. By then the exam days were almost up and I looked stressed and tense.

Chapter Six

Chennai Airport

Six days were left for the exam in London when I had vacated the Madras Medical Mission Guest House. It was on a Wednesday and the theory examination would be on the coming Tuesday.

Early in the morning, I met a few colleagues of the Madras Medical Mission seeking their wishes. The Sri Lankan Airlines flight to London was at 4 O'clock in the evening. After coming from the hospital I rechecked my travel documents. I looked for the new attire I had bought for the London journey, but alas, it was missing! I looked for it everywhere and the frantic searches got me jittery. In fact, after paying the bill I had forgotten to take it from the mall! My mind had been preoccupied with some sort of excitement and tension because of the coming day's travel. I must have gotten carried away while shopping.

There was no time left to get in touch with the shop I had bought it from. Disappointment and feelings of guilt clouded my spirits for a moment, but soon everything went away. I got ready shortly, clad in just an old pair of pants and a shirt!

As I made my way to the Chennai Airport in an auto rickshaw (the traditional three wheeler taxi in India), many thoughts daunted me. On top of them were the worries about my hand baggage of books that weighed an astounding 42 kilograms! The weight allowance for the hand baggage was only 7 kg and if I tried to put it along with the main baggage, it would surpass the weight limit I was allowed to carry.

I have had a penchant for books ever since I can remember. Reading up to the last minute before an exam was a habit, without which my confidence would be on shaky grounds. So there was no question of discarding these books. I was a bit nervous on the way to the airport. I could only hope that someone, either in the form of a passenger or an airport staff, would appear out of the blue like a miracle offering some form of help to carry these books. These sorts of hopes keep me moving always.

I knew from past experience that last minute rushes would be very uncomfortable for me and so I reached the airport at around 11:30 AM, well before the time. In fact the flight was at 7:00 PM and I was supposed to be at the airport by around 4:00 PM only.

The airport lounge was brightly lit and bustling with people moving hither, thither and yon. The check-in counter was not open yet. My eyes scanned through the passenger crowd, looking for a single face that might look familiar or anyone who looked appropriate enough to approach. I caught up with a lady who seemed to be a Sri Lankan, but she said she was only up to Colombo. After that I made random approaches to whoever I saw but it was of no use and I felt shaken. It had not struck me that I was asking something nobody would ever like to do.

The people around me were of different classes and had different intentions. Carrying something belonging to an unknown person would be quite risky to them, since it could even cost them their lives.

How could they know the real nature of my intentions?

So how could I blame them for their denial?

Right then however, my mind had no space for such justifications tinged with philosophy. I was simply selfish and my mind was focused on reaching the UK with all these books for study which was more important than anything else!

I spend about 4 hours in the airport. I was not able to see anyone who could offer me some help regarding my hand baggage. The check-in counter opened and a gigantic queue formed in a jiffy. Disappointed at not finding a way to solve the hand baggage issue, I stood waiting for my turn, expecting the worst and steering myself to face it.

Finally it was my turn. I submitted my documents to the officer at the check-in counter. While verifying my documents, I noticed an uneasy look flashing across his face. My heart skipped a beat. After a moment my passport and other documents were returned without a boarding pass!

I was not authorized to travel on that day because my name was not there on the list of confirmed passengers! I stood still for a moment with intense darkness filling my eyes, breaking out in cold sweat. When I got over the initial shock, I started to argue. I told the check-in officer that I am a doctor going to the UK for an important examination, for something very crucial in my life and "now only six days are left," I said, all in one breath. I was panting with sweat trickling down all over my body. I begged and in fact began to scream for some sort of help from him to travel the same day. He expressed his helplessness and I could read the sympathy from his face. He suggested contacting my travel agent who he alleged, was responsible for the mishap. Finally, I accepted the reality.

To put it retrospectively, I was moving through the different phases of a grieving process.

Soon I was on the phone talking to my travel agent, fuming with utter desperation. He seemed unresponsive and unable to understand my position and kept asserting that he had confirmed the ticket. He was taking all this in a lighter vein and refused to come to the airport. After a long heated exchange, I felt I was beginning to lose it. I told him how important the exam and the day were to me in my life. But nothing seemed to bother him. Finally I threatened him and put it across in rather strong words that he would face dire consequences if he failed me at once. I still don't know what had gotten into me to push me to such extremes.

At last he came to the airport. By then the check-in counter was empty and had closed already. The colorful crowd and the messy noises had all vanished. Only an eerie silence remained.

I was still enraged. He realized how serious my predicament was and went inside the office with my travel documents.

It was 7:10 PM, the departure time. The flight left as scheduled, leaving me in the lurch. I stood there gaping, unable to digest what had happened.

The travel agent returned after a while and I could sense a feeling of guilt smeared on his face. He clearly understood what state I was in and was really upset over his earlier attitude. He began to talk something serious with someone on his cell phone, a tad bit far from my hearing range. After that discussion he promised me that he would do everything he could to make sure that I could go as early as possible and apologized for his carelessness that had caused me so much trouble.

His name was Raju and his body language reassured me and somehow, hopes started budding again. I stopped panting.

It was night already. Raju helped me put my luggage in the cloakroom of the airport. I followed him along the Poonamallee High Road of Chennai, dragging my trolley handbag in the night to his manager's office. I felt no weariness or hunger amidst all this chaos. Finally we reached a hotel. Raju took me to a room inside where I saw a young man, maybe in his thirties sitting on a sofa. He was very fair and well built. He wore only half pants and a thick gold chain hung over his bare hairy chest. His tummy was large and disproportionate. In front of him, placed on a teapoy was a liquor bottle with a just trifle of liquor in it and a half-filled glass. A plate of cashew nuts was laid beside him right on the sofa. He seemed relaxed, reclining on the couch, stretching his right leg beside the teapoy. With a twitching motion of his wrist he was gently snacking on the nuts one after the other, while the other hand remained outstretched on the backrest of the couch.

He did not make any eye contact with me. Visibly irritated, he turned to Raju and asked, "Why have you brought him here at this hour?"

He seemed aware of the whole affair. Obviously Raju had briefed him on what had happened right from the airport. Yet, I could not understand the reason for his uneasiness in spite of all the troubles I had gone through just because of his office staff. Could it be that I was making a mess of his private hours?

His speech and behavior gave another jolt to my already traumatized mind.

That night I was given accommodation and food at a nearby hotel and I stayed there with an altogether disturbed mind.

What would I tell my wife and children?

I had promised to call them before boarding the flight and I knew my wife would be counting by the minute waiting for my call. This delay would only stir up the anxiety in her already clouded mind.

I called up the reception staff and asked them to connect me to my wife. My mind was fragmented. I had no idea what to tell her and how. I heard her sound at the other end of the line, which was very low and feeble, as if she was anticipating something bad. Suddenly I lost my control, and my emotions burst out. I was gasping for words. Loud sobs were heard at the other end, with my twin children joining in too. They were highly upset, even though unsure of what was going on. A few moments passed and then the storm began to settle. Slowly I narrated the story to her. She composed herself and tried to pacify me. I tried talking to my children, only to end up in tears. I had simply lost my balance in an amalgam of mixed feelings.

The next day, Thursday in the afternoon, Raju bought another flight ticket through a different travel service at his expense. So he paid for his mistake. He had done his best to keep his promise. By then I had lost two valuable pre-exam days out of six. The theory examination was scheduled for the next Tuesday. I went to the airport early in the morning on Friday and collected the luggage I had left at the cloakroom two days ago. The flight was at 10 am, via Bahrain.

The outcome of the hand baggage routine began to nag my mind and I took up the hunt once more with the waiting passengers. The upshot was an instant replay of the last time. I soon got the boarding pass and the main luggage got through without any hitches. The check-in officer just took a casual look at my hand baggage and made no comments. I gave out a huge sigh of relief and felt like stepping into an air-conditioned room from the blazing hot sun, but the feeling wasn't for long. I was caught!

There was another officer around, who was looking into these matters. He noticed that my handbag was bulging out on all the sides. He lifted it up to see how heavy it was. I was on pins and needles again. In a state of helplessness, I felt I was being pushed to one side and losing my balance.

His fierce look with the baring teeth reminded me of some scary growling beast. Suspiciously, he asked me what the

CHAPTER SEVEN

Heathrow Airport

It was Saturday, 8 O'clock in the morning. The sky looked dim and cloudy, the sun was not to be seen anywhere.

I had landed at the Heathrow Airport. The new place and new people evoked some excitement. So impressive was the airport ambience.

The airport had always been a place of mixed feelings, where everyone would be anxious to go somewhere. Lots of hugs and kisses would be exchanged. Some were leaving and others were reunited with their loved ones and friends. Everywhere there were vibrant emotions. I did not look at the waiting crowd outside, as I was not expecting anyone. In fact, I cannot remember anyone close to me ever accompanying me to see me off on any of my travels, nor have I ever been received at the airport.

I was entering another country with new opportunities awaiting me. I came out, pushing my trolley along and glanced at my watch. It was 9:00 AM already. Though it was summer season, I felt really cold outside. It was my first visit to the United Kingdom and I had not taken any proper clothing to face the country's weather. There was neither any proper planning for my journey nor was there anyone to guide me on such matters.

I looked for a place to sit down and relax, roaming around the airport with my trolley and then sat on a bench that was nearly frozen. The frost of the metal bench pierced through my lean body like sharp spikes. My jaws and teeth started to chatter. I felt absolutely miserable. The long hours of flight without proper sleep and the unaccustomed food I was served on the way made things worse. I sat there fiddling with some coins and thoughts about my next step began to run in my mind. Saturday and Sunday are the weekend holidays in the UK and no bank would be open to encash the demand draft I had with me. In fact I was supposed to land here on Thursday if the unforeseen incidents had not occurred at the Chennai Airport.

How to survive the next two days with the remaining eight pounds was bugging me continuously, only to be interrupted by my growling stomach. I attempted to get a hold of the person I had met through the internet. He had offered me a cheap and affordable stay in East Ham London, where a bunch of Indians, especially Keralites lived.

There was no response from the other end of the phone. I lost 4 one pound coins in those unsuccessful attempts. I was putting in a one pound coin every time unknowingly, where actually some pence would have sufficed! All alone in my venture, I had to endure my blunders standing out because of my poor planning.

At the next turn, I heard his voice half asleep. He was resting after his night shift work. I apologized for interrupting his sleep and felt reluctant to continue the talk. My further efforts to stay on at least till my theory examination depended on the help he would hopefully offer. I was totally at the receiving end and did not like to start on the wrong foot with him. So I got an appointment to contact him later at his convenience and hung up the phone.

He was a rank stranger to me and I had no idea about his whereabouts or his nature. Indeed, he had his roots in Kerala, my home state, but I had not made any attempt to find out more before starting out on my journey.

I felt so sad and disappointed. Yet the good news was that he remembered me all the same and even the emails I had sent him. I was badly in need of a shelter to evade the freezing cold at the airport and time was running out.

I spent a pound on a simple breakfast and this time managed to get hold of three one-pound coins as change. I had no idea when I could contact him again, or how long I would have to wait at the airport. In any case, this person was the only hope I had then.

Hoping for the best, I tried to catch some sleep on a bench using my bag as a headrest. I rolled myself up like a dog to maintain the warmth of my torso and the posture made me feel compassionate towards myself. I was losing precious time for a final round of preparation for the exam and I was absolutely helpless. However, there was one thing that still kept me on and that was my burning desire to appear for the exam and come out with flying colours.

I could not sleep, lying like the way I was on the bench and my mind was all alert. I saw through my closed eyes, the post-exam euphoria of relief and the happiness of my family within my hand's reach. My feelings and emotions began to sublimate giving warmth to my frozen mind. The moments became lighter and lighter, slowly acquiring a not-so-unpleasant buoyancy which carried me to a blissful state . . .

It was past midday when I opened my eyes. I made a quick stop to see if my personal belongings were all in the right place and made another attempt on the phone. This time my friend was fully awake and he briefed me about my stay in East Ham and his terms and conditions. He gave me directions too, to reach the place.

But how could I reach there?

I knew nothing about the city and did not know anyone else there except this guy. He had no idea what state I was in at the airport. I gave him a brief idea of my situation especially since I was penny less and also the difficulty I was facing with my demand draft because of the bank holiday. He stated it would be difficult to pick me up from the airport that afternoon. It was a 150 kilometer drive from his residence and moreover, he had to come to the airport at 9 O'clock on the same night anyway to pick up his family coming from Dubai in the Middle East. He wanted to avoid the unnecessary expenditure and strain too. It all sounded very reasonable, but for me, it meant waiting at the airport for another nine hours! Yet I was in no position to make any demands and I settled down for the long wait. Altogether it was going to be a twelve hour wait at the airport!

The coins I had would not suffice for a square meal. All this physical exhaustion did not hamper me mentally, but it did concern me whether I would run into hypoglycemia (a state of low blood sugar, resulting in loss of consciousness temporarily) as I was diabetic. I had to survive for another 8-9 hours without risking hypoglycemia. I took tea with sugar in between, though it was not my usual practice. Long hours lay ahead of me, like a never-ending road and I did not know how to kill time. I was in no mood to open my books until and unless I resolved myself. I just sat there; the darkness began to descend reminding me that time was ticking away.

My friend came to the airport at 8:30 PM and found me without much difficulty. The destitute and nervous state of my mind must have showed up on my face, as he was easily able to spot me among the small crowd at the airport.

I made no comments on what I had gone through over the last twelve hours, stranded over there. During our little talk over the phone, something about his attitude had become clear to me: he did not want me to take any advantage over the fact that we were Keralites and I was keen not to do so. So our meeting was a very formal one.

CHAPTER EIGHT

East Ham. London

At about 11:00 PM, he dropped me at the place where I was to stay. It was a three bedroom villa. His parents were staying there and they had gone to Kerala on a vacation. The chap was obviously attempting to get a small earning during their absence. He pointed out the dos and don'ts while staying at the house along with the terms and conditions. The rent of fifty pounds a week was affordable to me.

My room was upstairs and seemed quite secure with ample ventilation. The light brown, room sized swirly carpet embellished the look and served an aura of warmth and comfort. However, there was no table or desk and the wardrobe was locked.

Through the glass window on one side, I could see an array of shining street lights with its large halo standing out in the darkness. The road was rather empty, with houses on both sides and the cars parked in front.

The room heater was making a feeble sound but annoying nonetheless, yet I felt a comforting ambience around me. The bed was well arranged appearing to be quite cozy. Under the king size comforter I laid, totally relaxed. All my exhaustion, weariness and hunger soon started to vanish, allowing my mind to rest in bliss, only to slip into a sound sleep.

It was a Sunday morning. It looked a bit brighter than the previous day. Again, I could not see the bright sun anywhere in the sky. Gradually I fell out of the hangover of the nightlong dead sleep. Instead of the sun, hunger began to scorch my insides. I had the regular morning pill for my diabetes. All through yesterday I had not eaten anything except for two or three cups of coffee and all that was left with me now was ninety pence! I sensed imminent danger. I tried to get in touch with my friend on his cell phone number which he had given me to use in case of emergencies. I was allowed to use the landline in the house and tried ringing him up. But there was no response. I feared the convulsions due to low blood sugar and my mind alluded to a dreadful experience I once had.

Swaraj Round is a known roundabout in Trichur (a district in Kerala state famous for its cultural heritage) always bustling with hectic traffic. Once I was in the middle of the busy road trying to cross to the other side. I had taken my regular anti-diabetic pill, but had not eaten any breakfast. I had just walked all the way from my residence to the Round. Suddenly I felt an unusual twitching in my eyelids. Slowly my eyes got covered in darkness, and I foresaw the inevitable danger that was approaching. I was about to lose my balance and control. My feeble cry for help did not elicit any response from the passersby, and I finally collapsed on the road. I lost consciousness for a moment, however I was cognizant of the movements in my body from the jerky motion of my jaws to the violent shaking of my limbs.

I was having severe convulsions. Someone was trying to place a metallic rod into my closed fist, a traditional practice believed to stop convulsions. Many thought I was an epileptic going through one of my phases.

When I opened my eyes, I was lying on the verandah of a herbal medicine shop. I saw the vendor looking at me sympathetically. I requested him to give me tea or a little sugar and he looked surprised. After taking some sugar my eyes became bright and I was on my feet again. I did not divulge who I was, but he must have read the gratitude in my eyes. He refused to accept money for the tea. Later on another day, I introduced my family to him when we happened to go past his shop.

Now, alone in the house of a stranger, these recollections of an unpleasant memory were giving me the jitters. My theory exam was in two days. I could not imagine another episode of hypoglycemia and convulsions and that too when I was alone. Settling my appetite became my utmost priority.

I had no ideas what I could get for the remaining ninety pence. I peeped out through the window; the streets were already awake, busy with the exuberance of life. I couldn't find any shops in my proximity.

Outside, I walked a few yards down the stone paved sidewalk to find a shop. It was a bakery. Quite a lot of items, most of them very unfamiliar and expensive, were displayed on the cabinet. I was looking for something I could get for the little money I had, but all I managed to get was a loaf of bread. The dry bread with a glass of water did not seem palatable to me, but I gulped it down some way.

Now, what would I do for lunch, the same bread and water?

I called up my friend and told him that I was running short of money terribly and explained the difficulty I had with cashing my DD this time owing to the weekend holidays. I also gave a brief description of the unexpected events at the Chennai Airport that had caused all this trouble. All I got in response was a dead silence, and I was unable to make out what was going on his mind.

Anyway, right then my priority was to survive and I made a strong effort to wriggle myself out of the shell of dignity and pride. I told him that I had not had any proper meal for the last 30 hours and that I was starving and diabetic. Any gesture of solace or kindness, either in words or emotions still seemed too expensive for him and a frozen silence resumed. I requested him to lend me 50 pounds, which I would return the very next morning as soon as the bank opened. He did not answer my request, but said in a noncommittal way that he would come over in the afternoon. I did not lose my confidence. In all my helplessness a dashing streak of light that resembled strength used to fill up my inner core from a source unknown. This strength always propelled me further.

He did not show up in the afternoon and this did not surprise me a bit.

I had not opened my books yet, and all that was left was one more day. The exam was scheduled for the day after the next. If at all he did not turn up by night, I decided to survive on bread and water. I had to help and save myself. I tried to console myself that at the maximum, I would have to go through this suffering only till the next morning when the banks would open.

Like the pleasant tunes of a harp soothing the draught mind was the news about my wife's younger sister. I was told by my wife that she was the University topper in the graduate level of examination that year.

My friend came with his wife at around half past six in the evening. He looked indifferent, as if he was not aware of anything I had told him and there wasn't any response from his side. I repeated the same story and showed him the DD. All this effort of mine was only to fill my stomach, fearing another dreaded episode of hypoglycemia and convulsion.

I saw him skewing at his wife, looking for the green light from her. Could it be that I had only seen the tip of the iceberg thus far? The moment I withdrew my gaze from the couple, he pulled a small folder paper from his trouser pocket and gave it to me, which after some unfolding turned out to be a 50 pound note!

Minutes after the couple left, I hurried to the street. I had not eaten anything except the dried bread and water for the past 40 hours. This time I was looking for a shop where I could get something more satisfying.

I walked past restaurants of different kind. Each one had a distinctive aroma surrounding it. Suddenly my eyes grew wide with excitement as I came across an Indian shop where I found the very dish I was particularly fond of ever since my childhood, differing only slightly in size and color. The steam cake which we used to make at home was brown in color, as it was made of brown rice flour and it was of medium size too.

That night I felt comfortable, physically and mentally. Only one day was left now for the theory examination. The coming morning I finished my business with the bank and made a survey of the route map to determine the location of the venue for the examination. All that was possible now was a quick glance over the books, with the limited time I had.

The theory examination, however, was a walkover and went smoothly. The next was the practical session which was very critical and would determine everything. I lay down in my bed, staring at the cloudy sky through the window.

What next, was the big question ahead of me.

There were around 45 days left for the practical examination. I neither knew anything about the hospitals in the UK, nor the patients. Many things, especially factors linked to cultural differences matter in the practical examination. It is purely performance based unlike the theory exam where all that you had to encounter was a question paper. I was getting very nervous. How did the children of this country look like?

What would be their customs and manners? What should be my methods of approach during the clinical examination?

Many thoughts marched through my head like a slide show.

The experiences some of my seniors had during their examination in the UK were quite concerning. What mattered here was not merely a factual knowledge of the subject. There were many other things that might appear silly to others yet had been critical for the exam. If the practical examination happened to be somewhere in Scotland, things would get more difficult. I had real concerns about the way I spoke English and my friends and seniors in Malaysia had warned me to take care in this regard. If I had difficulty in understanding the Scottish slang, the whole thing would end up in smoke. All these thoughts were stressful indeed.

Ever since I started my journey, situations somehow shape out to be incisive and challenging and priorities kept on changing.

Thus my next priority was to find out a clinical attachment in a hospital in London. A thorough clinical preparation, a rehearsal of the proceedings and getting used to the unfamiliar hospital system were all vital to perform well in the practical exam.

But how would I go about this?

Where would I start?

My head seemed to be muddled. I had nobody to contact, no strings to pull and no godfather to help and guide me. Two uneventful days had passed after the theory examination and 43 days remained. I could not find any way to sort out the problem and my mind had fallen into a state of total blackout.

At last I decided to visit the Edinburgh Royal Victoria Infirmary Hospital. I had received word that one of my classmates of the postgraduate days in India had a teaching job there. I did not have his contact details, yet I thought that by visiting him personally, he might be able to guide me or recommend me to some Pediatric Chiefs for a clinical attachment in any other hospital. I had not had any contact with him after our postgraduate days and I was not quite sure if he would be helpful at all. An idea began to lighten my spirits: suppose I could not find him or he turned away from my request, I could just meet the department heads and lay my request before each and every one of them. I would knock on every available door till the last one opened for me.

The next morning I went to the railway station and missed the train to Edinburgh by five minutes. The next train was only after two hours. I was feeling quite impatient and restless and went on a search for an internet café to utilize my time effectively. There was one a few yards away. I had not checked my mail for days.

There were quite a few mails in my mailbox, but one in particular caught my attention.

I had not heard anything about Dr Fiona Trail for some time, and memories of her had started to fade. I had seen her for the first time at the Physical Medicine Clinic of CMC Vellore, a very lean, short lady with a native British accent. Dr Fiona and her husband were attached to some sort of a sponsored program at CMC and attended the clinic regularly. She used to smile in a diplomatic casual style and I always felt that she liked to keep a distance.

In fact I was a bit reluctant to volunteer. Some of my childhood complexities had become a part of me and they still are, to an extent. But our regular meetings at the physical medicine clinic and the academic discussions had made me a little more confident to talk liberally to her. She was from Newcastle upon Tyne in the UK and I found it difficult to believe that she was a consultant in physical medicine working in the UK. She appeared very simple, and much less sophisticated than I had believed her to be.

One day I received a chance to open my mind and I asked her if it would be possible for me to find a clinical attachment in any of the hospitals in the UK. I was just seeking her guidance, but she did not respond in the way I had expected. She just listened to me silently and after a momentary pause, said in a cool and casual way that she would look into it and then left abruptly.

Disappointed, I decided to forget about the incident and went along with my efforts to find other alternatives. Soon I finished my program in the physical medicine department and shifted to another department since I was on rotation attending the various departments of interest in CMC. I saw Dr Fiona Trail later on two occasions on the campus, but I felt she was just ignoring me. I could not understand why she behaved like that and I was not much interested to know either.

One day, I received an email from her.

What had she written to me now?

What did she want to tell me?

I never expected any sort of communication from her and how did she come to have my email address in the first place?

Intriguing!

Then I remembered that I had given her a one-page resume when I had presented my topic. She had then not seemed to have any interest in it. I was certain however, that this mail bore with it an offer of assistance. The initial curiosity was replaced by an anxious expectation of something big. My heart beat faster with every click of the computer mouse as I opened the mailbox. The content was short and precise to the point:

"GO TO NEWCASTLE GENERAL HOSPITAL AND MEET Dr WILLIAM FRASER ALEXANDER. HE WILL ARRANGE EVERYTHING FOR YOU."

Regards,
Fiona Trail.

Just two simple sentences.

But to me under the circumstances, the message had a skyrocketing effect with tons of energy to boost me up!

For a moment I stood numb.

Adrenaline pumped into my blood, my hair follicles erupting as if cold water was running over them. I couldn't control my emotions and I found people in the café staring at me. I was in fact carried away by my feelings and I even forgot to send a reply to Dr Fiona Trail. She had indeed done something great. I regretted the way I had underestimated her. She might have been stingy with words and expressions, but she was generous at heart. My confidence had risen and I walked with firm and heavy footsteps, like a warrior who had just won a battle. I cancelled the ticket to Edinburgh and returned to my room. Soon I met my friend, settled all the dues and vacated the room. Even though some painful feelings still lingered in my mind, I tried to put a smile on my face throughout my interactions.

The next morning I set out for Newcastle. I contacted the Newcastle General Hospital from the railway station and was able to talk with Dr William Fraser Alexander. I was really pleased with the way he greeted me, and he was speaking as if we had been acquainted with each other for a long time. I guess Dr Fiona had probably given him a good brief about me.

CHAPTER NINE

Newcastle General Hospital, Newcastle upon Tyne

I reached the hospital at around 12:30 PM. The day started out warm and sunny. As my taxi cab sped away, I took a quick glimpse around. The hospital looked so different in structure from those I had seen in India and Malaysia. The full-length glass windows and the entrance reminded me of an antique cuckoo clock. The premises were paved with concrete tiles quite neatly. In the centre, there were thick bushes of different colours encircled by a lawn of carpeted green grass. The pine trees and the outdoor lightings added to the elegance, making the whole structure look like a historical monument from the medieval times.

The atmosphere seemed quite silent. A few cars and vans could be seen along with some people, patients probably, moving here and there. I started to move slowly, dragging my trolley along, to the main entrance. Opposite me a few meters away on the other side, I saw an English gentleman standing

41

as if waiting for someone. He was dressed in white shirt and pants, with a black belt on the waist that revealed his torso. It seemed that he was moving towards me and I backed up to look around. There was no one else there. I was sure that he was looking at me. As I drew closer to him, I saw the alert face give out an innocent smile. He looked younger than I had figured from the distance. There was a sense of pleasure in him to see the person who he was waiting for. I was trying hard to cover up my confusion instead.

He greeted me and introduced himself. After reassuring him that I was the same person he was looking for, he explained to me that he was from the accommodation office of the Newcastle General Hospital. He was deputed to receive me and take me to my accommodation.

For an instant I stood there transfixed, unable to believe myself! Things had been organized beyond my imagination and expectation, but by whom and how, remained a question. I could feel the smooth transition of events, from the Chennai Airport to Heathrow to Newcastle. Joy, happiness and excitement burst like sparkling fireworks and a newfound confidence was brimming inside me.

He helped me carry my luggage into the van and then drove me to my place of stay. He left after giving me a handshake and greetings in typical British manner. My eyes were teary. I simply smiled at him and could not utter a word! I stood there gasping for words, feeling numb all over. I thanked the Almighty for his kindness.

Dr Fiona's sister, who was in the UK, had made some unofficial enquiries on my behalf with the accommodation officer, Mrs Margaret Tyson. Dr Fiona Trail had replied once for my email, but I hadn't received any message ever since.

I started my clinical attachment job at the Newcastle General Hospital. It was a different atmosphere altogether, with new people, a different culture and a new system. Being authorized for a clinical attachment to the hospital, I now had free access to the Royal Victoria Infirmary and the

Freeman Hospital which were within two kilometers reach and I could make free use of the shuttle bus service that connected them.

I shaved off my mustache and became clean-shaven for the first time in my life. I was under the impression that examiners in the UK might not like a mustache. I was well informed right from my days in Malaysia about the dress code a candidate had to pursue during the exam. I was keen not to create any sort of negative impression with my body language and the way I dressed. I knew that taking off the mustache just before the exam would certainly bar my self-esteem, so I decided to take it away much earlier in order to get accustomed to my new appearance. Though it felt strange to me at first, I soon got used to it.

The entire environment was new too. I had some hiccups adjusting to the system, yet I learned from every mistake I made. Every day was a new day with new children and their different medical problems. I used to read a lot in libraries and attend several seminars, clinical presentations, discussions, mock viva sessions and tutorials at different hospitals, one after the other. My academic caliber began to expand in all dimensions.

Two other doctors also in clinical attachment along with me were Dr Mustapha from Iraq and Dr Zeenath from Bangladesh. I was the self-assigned group leader to organize and coordinate the teaching programs for us. My daily schedules were busy and exhaustive. I was enjoying each and every minute of that life. Meanwhile, to my relief, Mrs Margaret Tyson reduced my rental fee from 75 to 40 Pounds per month. Dr Alexander had put in a word in my favor. He was very helpful and encouraging too. So were the specialist registrars (the job title for junior specialist doctors) who worked under him.

My kinship with everyone in the hospital was purely of a pedantic nature focused totally on my goals. In that respect, my family too was out of my focus most of the time.

I cannot recall when I met Ewa for the first time. She was from Poland and was a specialist registrar working under Dr Alexander. She was more considerate to me than the other registrars. When she invited me to her house for the first time, I was a bit surprised even though I did not express it. After all, I belonged to the so called third world, so what was so special about me?

I was still not free from the binds of the complexes that ruled my thinking process.

Ewa introduced me to her husband Dr Posner, a young British doctor and their children. One of them, Thomas was hardly one year and the elder Daniel, around four years old. Dr Posner did his practice privately. He was amiable and diplomatic too. Ewa was very much excited to talk about her children and husband, a very caring mother and wife at the same time.

I have lost count of the number of times she invited me to her house. She cooked delicious food for me every time and I relished it. It was a respite from my monotonous food habits.

I still had financial constraints. I did not have any source of income in Newcastle and I had to spend wisely. Most of the time, I survived with bread and peanut butter only. At times, I used to cook with the others in the hostel.

Once, Ewa gave me a nice sweater as a gift. Though I was reluctant to consent, she used to insist me on making an international call to my house from her landline. Each time I left her house, it became part of her routine to give me takeaway food packs and drop me by the hostel. On one occasion there was a 10 pound currency note carefully kept in the food pack!

At times I wondered if she had a sixth sense in understanding my difficulties. Later on, I gathered enough confidence and asked her about her past. She had faced the same kind of difficulties and struggles as I did when she came to the UK for the first time. Those hardships might have broadened her mind to accommodate any oddities. Time was moving fast and only two weeks were left for the practical examination. After that the ordeal would be over! The initial enthusiasm and euphoria had given way to surmounting stress and tension. I had to be selective about my shuttle between hospitals. A fine-tuning of the process was necessary.

One day, I suddenly started feeling exhausted and feverish. My body was ailing with intense headaches and backaches and I was feeling itchy all over. What was happening to me all of a sudden? For the first time after starting my attachment program, I took leave and rested for a full day, feeling too uncomfortable to read or do anything else.

I tried to console myself thinking that it would be some sort of viral fever; took some symptomatic medication and slept through the whole day and night. The next day I felt even more tired and uneasy. I was certain that something was happening to me out of the blue! My fingernails were stained with blood due to the continuous scratching on my head and the pills for itching didn't seem to do the job.

My God . . . !

Was all lost at the last minute?

Only thirteen days were left for the practical examination. What I had feared and prayed not to happen was happening right before me! I was sure I would not recover fully from this curse well before my examination.

What next then?

I could not imagine another go at the examination.

How would I meet the expenses in the first place? What about the visa?

What would I tell my wife and children?

I felt like being thrown into the abyss once again.

Had I made that narrow escape from the Chennai Airport only to lose it all in the UK at the end?

I was unable to think rationally.

To whom would I talk?

I was floppy and carried away by the tsunami of emotions.

God, is there an end to this?

How long are you going to test me like this?

I knew such questions stem out of sheer desperation and helplessness. The underlying reason is the lack of confidence to face adversities in life and I was not one to fall for that. So I made all effort to regain my sense of balance.

The roaring waves of emotions slowly began to subside. Bubbles of positive thoughts began to surface slowly, one after the other. I have always been lucky that way and I always got the energy and vitality for further darting.

My mind was still fertile. As the dense dark clouds began to disappear, new hopes began to bud.

It took nearly fifteen days for me to make a full recovery from chicken pox, my malady and those were the tough days. I was confined to my room. On occasions, I would open the front door, make sure that all the inmates had gone to the hospital, and head to the kitchen. Dr Abdul, a fellow inmate from Tamil Nadu was of great help. He was very kind and used to cook for me during my days of illness.

I would wait eagerly for the knock on the door after his return from the hospital. After the knock, he would slowly push the food tray into my room through the gap under the main door. It reminded me of some films I had seen, where condemned criminals were given food through peepholes in the slammer! Yet there was a difference, since we couldn't see each other. I would not open the door so that he wouldn't be exposed to my chicken pox. With another knock he would go away. It was just a silent understanding, with no prior planning. We stood on either side of the door, bonded by the spirit of our minds which were beyond my apprehension. This routine went on for about two weeks.

The chicken pox was over. I had now the looks of a battered soldier with marks and burrows all over my body and the one on the forehead was a bit deep. I smelled even worse. I had missed my long-awaited precious examination, and I had to surrender to destiny. I was suddenly thrown to the bottom square, like in a game of snakes and ladders and today I had to start from scratch!

And to make matters worse, I did not have anyone dear to me at that time to share my feelings. My wife was seriously ill and admitted in a hospital in India. My children were taken care of by their grandparents. It was the first time that they were living without their parents. They were hardly ten years old then and felt very insecure and uncomfortable. Both of them started to weep when I got to them over the phone. It was really a hard time for all of us.

I somehow managed to contact my wife who was in a critical state, but did not disclose anything about myself. She was in a dilemma herself. She could not tell anything about me to her parents or siblings, as they had not been informed about my actual whereabouts. As far as they knew, I was still in Malaysia!

The next exam was after four months. I had so many things to settle before planning to give it another shot. The most important of them was the extension of my visa, which I learnt should not be a problem as long as Dr Alexander was there for support. The next priority was money. I had some pounds remaining in my account which I had saved by penny-pinching. I would never again dine outside, survived on bread and peanut butter and walked whenever possible instead of spending on transport. But whatever I had in the bank was just sufficient for the examination fee, but how was I to meet the expenses for my stay here and for the other related needs too?

I had absolutely no idea. I tried hard to find some part-time job, but that did not work out because of the legal issues related to my visa status. Anyway, I was determined not to lose heart or else I would not have progressed to where I stand today. I made a decision deep in my mind to survive no matter what with whatever money I had. If I got broke I would borrow money from some friends as the last but the inevitable consequence.

As a matter of relief, a doctor of Indian descent who worked as a consultant gave me assurance of financial help in case I got into trouble. Meanwhile, my return ticket was postponed till further notice. So I made essential arrangements to stay for another four months. I received official permission to resume the clinical attachment program and this was mandatory because chickenpox poses risk to sick children and the public. I got lots of help from the people around me and particularly Ewa. She gave me considerable emotional support. Once she took me to the beach with her children. The time I spent with Ewa at her house on Christmas Eve was particularly memorable. Eventually, I came back to my usual routine.

The examination was in the month of February. With hardly a month left, I had not realized how fast time was flying. I forgot all about the immediate past and focused my attention on studies and the forthcoming exam. I survived most of the day on nothing but bread and peanut butter. I kept consoling myself that all my hard times were coming to an end soon.

The schedules for the practical exam were officially released. This time the examination was to be held in the General Hospital of Kirkcaldy in Glasgow the next Monday and after that, I would be flying back to India from London! Anticipation of the ecstatic moments propelled me further. I made it a point to have my return air ticket reconfirmed, to avoid another Chennai episode. Meanwhile, new worries started to settle in.

The English accent in Glasgow is different from the other regions of England. The practical examination is very much time bound and any difficulty in effective communication with my patients and caretakers would hamper my rapport with them which was critical to the outcome of the examination.

Why should I feel anxious about those things unnecessarily?

What was left, after all?

And what was I going to lose in the end?

Over the last eight months, my life had been stumbling over humps and gutters that fragmented my aspirations and ambitions into pieces.

The never ending cat and mouse game was still going on . . .

Was everything that had happened so far, and all that were about to happen just for my good? Soon my negative thoughts swept away and my mind replenished itself with new energy and vigor. The countdown had started and three more days were left for the exam. I reserved a train ticket to Kirkcaldy, which was rather far from Newcastle upon Tyne, towards the northern side of the United Kingdom. I had to start a day in advance, and needed to make arrangements for an overnight stay there. By then I had collected some details of B&B in Kirkcaldy. B&B is the short for Bed-and-Breakfast, a system that provides overnight stay and breakfast. I made an advance booking at one close to the Kirkcaldy railway station for 25 UK pounds and that was the cheapest available.

The next matter was the suit to wear for the examination. The dress code was very important and I was never used to such formal attires and did not like it as well due to some ideologies. A new one would cost me around 150-250 pounds which was pretty hefty. Through Dr Fiona Trail, I came to know about the charity shops in the UK where I could get a variety of secondhand things at cheap rates. People donated used things they no longer wanted in these charity shops. Sometimes, I was told, the belongings of the people who were no more were also kept there to be sold at reasonable prices for charity activities. Even then, I felt undeterred.

I found one at a walking distance from the hospital. At that time, distances that many felt long were only strolls for me! That way, I managed to save a little bit of money too. A secondhand suit cost me only 5 pounds. It looked cute and it was more than enough for a one-day use.

Everything was ready now. I organized my carry bag, making sure that all the necessary books, dresses, documents, etc. were in place. I checked and double checked. The exam was the day after the following day! Anxiety was building up. The next morning, I prepared my food pack consisting of the usual bread and peanut butter for lunch and dinner and a bottle full of water kept ready in the bag.

The train reached Kirkcaldy at around 5:30 in the evening. The sun began to set and the night with its freshness and beauty was falling in. The B&B I had booked was quite close to the station.

The B&B is a good arrangement and an additional source of income for a family. Sometimes it could be the principal source of income for many. A few rooms may be less than ten were converted into an abode for an affordable stay. The owners themselves made the breakfast and did the housekeeping chores as well. The facility was available everywhere, a real blessing for those who cannot afford expensive hotel stay. I got in touch with the Kirkcaldy Hospital to confirm its location and distance from my place. The hospital was hardly 4-5 km from the B&B. Once again I checked to make sure that everything would be in order for the next day. I felt more relaxed. Since I had made the final revisions on the train, I did not feel like reading anymore. Afterwards I took a shower with hot water. The room was comfortably warm. The physical exhaustion of the day and the dead silence around soon put me to sleep.

CHAPTER TEN

General Hospital Kirkcaldy. Scotland

I woke up very early in the morning, well before the set time of the alarm in my cell phone which I carried with me all the time without a SIM card.

I had received instructions to be present at the examination hall by 8:00 AM sharp. I wanted to be there much earlier than the specified time since I always felt comfortable that way.

I got ready by 5:30 AM. There was a bus stop quite close to where I stayed, to get to Kirkcaldy Hospital. The bus ride would take less than half an hour, and so I would be there well before time. I needed plenty of time at hand so that I would be able to fend off any unexpected delays.

I did a final round of checking. I looked for a small bag in which I had kept my stethoscope, a small knee hammer and a few other things—the essential tools for the clinical examination of patients. I searched for it everywhere inside the large carry bag and outside as well, even though I was sure I had not opened the carry bag at all after I left Newcastle.

I could not find it anywhere. I had my heart in my mouth. I was sure I had put everything I needed for the clinical examination in that small bag.

But did I misplace the bag itself finally?

Cursing myself, I squatted down on the floor, covering my face with both my palms in reflex. I was ashamed of myself for my carelessness.

Everything went black for a fraction of a second. Of course, this was not the way candidates usually go to face an examination. Everyone would be comfortable to use things that they are used to, rather than experimenting with something new, especially during an exam. I did not continue to let myself down, as time was very crucial. I thought I would borrow those items from the hospital, and tried to maintain my composure.

6:10 AM

It was already ten past six in the morning. I had to be in the hospital by seven at all costs. I settled the bills for my B&B, and stepped out of the main door.

It was morning of course, but looking outside I was not able to feel the usual freshness and fragrance of a morning. I could not see anything around me. Everything was covered in snow. The sky looked cloudy and tinted with a thick fog. All the lavish green I had seen yesterday had vanished completely, to be blanketed with a thick carpet of snow!

I had seen snow in Newcastle. My body used to get covered head to toe with snow, at times making me even look like a polar bear. Icy crystals would fall with a faint tapping sound on my nose between my face and glasses. Whenever it fell on the tip of my tongue, I tried to taste it! The tall fig trees with frozen leaves looked desolate and silent. There were no more of the chirping and tweeting.

The crystal clear water drops soon turned into tiny glass balls and the dangling leaves held onto it with a mysterious smile against the cold wind that was trying to snatch it.

The nature and its beauty were snowing on my scorched mind during my stressful days there and I enjoyed it very much. Winter was a new experience for me as I had never seen it before.

Yesterday's relentless snowing made life stand still everywhere, oblivious to me as I was sound asleep.

The roofs of the terraced houses, the doors and windows were snow-clad beyond recognition. The phone boxes and the trees were all blanketed in white. The roads had become impassable, covered with snow several inches deep. Cars and vans stood in front of the houses, all covered in snow. I could see very faintly, workers trying to open the road with shovels. Virtually, there wasn't any movement at all. Life had come to a standstill. The temperature had plummeted to below zero degrees Celsius, and there I was in just a shirt and suit.

How would I get to the bus stop?

6:20 AM

Sooner or later I was sure to run short of time. I had so far not been able to take one step ahead from where I had started. At last I made up my mind; I would walk up to the bus stop, hoping to get some sort of transportation there. As I guided my footsteps, my leg sunk deep into the snow; when I lifted it out with great difficulty, the other leg would already be buried in the inches deep snow, reminding me of walking in a muddy paddy field back home. Particles of snow settled between my shoes and socks literally chilling me in the bones. A very uncomfortable and a difficult experience ensued, as I was quite new to such weather conditions. I felt totally helpless, like a toddler.

7:15 AM

A few people stood at the bus stop, and I found them wearing snow boots. They were all well adapted to the situation. I was wearing only a pair of casual shoes. I was really, really exhausted. My suit was fully covered with snow and had lost its luster and freshness. Looking at it, I got really sad and dejected. Maybe I should not have started in a full suit.

I took off the suit and wiped off all the snow covering it, folded and covered it with a newspaper to carry it in my hand. I certainly was passing through a difficult time, as usual!

8:00 AM

The exam was scheduled to start at 8:00 AM by the dot. The road was still covered with snow. I could not see any vehicles except a few gritting lorries and snow plows trying to open the road. There was absolutely no sign of any form of transport. No buses, cars or taxis. Time was running short and tension was mounting, like the snow in front of me. I struggled to keep myself from panicking.

I decided to get in touch with the Kirkcaldy Hospital so that I could inform them about the state I was in and request for some form of transport if possible. It seemed to be the only sensible thing to do in the situation. There was a public telephone box close by. I reached out for my purse, but could not find it in the back pocket of my pants where I always kept it. I checked everywhere, but the purse was not to be seen.

Did I leave it in my room?

A walk back to the B&B?

Unthinkable, yet there was no other way. I had to undergo the hard ordeal of walking through the slush again, but the purse was not to be found! And then it hit me. All this time the purse was actually in the pocket of my suit, which I was carrying covered by the newspaper! Such errors do always trail me like a shadow in challenging and stressful situations.

From the B&B, I contacted the Kirkcaldy Hospital, but they expressed with regret their helplessness in those conditions.

A walk to the bus stop again?

Three waddles through the slush in total.

After the first time, I guess we become more experienced to brave the walks that followed.

Each second was valuable and precious now, and yet things were slipping away from my grip. It was 9:10 AM. The exam might well have begun, and here I was trapped in a bus stop, in a terribly helpless situation.

I felt so pathetic about my current state, especially when the long and eagerly awaited exam was at the door step.

Chicken pox had already scarred my dream once; had it stuck again this time in the form of deadly snow?

I took a mental decision not to give up at any cost and fight against all odds and adversities with my willpower.

11:00 AM

Gradually, the day became sunnier. I could see at least more people around now.

Slowly, one or two vehicles began to surface on the road, crawling along through it. I tried to hitchhike in one of the vehicles I saw, but it was not in the direction of Kircaldy Hospital.

Taxi drivers were not willing to go towards the Kirkcaldy side because of the poor road conditions in that area and I missed two or three cabs for this reason. Finally I was able to convince a taxi driver. The condition of the road was still miserable, and he could only move very slowly, and at last dropped me some 200 meters away from the hospital as he was not able to advance further. Finally I managed to get myself to the hospital at 11:30 AM. I did not have any hope that I would be allowed to take the examination after that sort of unpardonable delay. Walking in at 11:30 AM instead of at 8 in the morning would not be acceptable for such an important examination.

Yet I was not deterred. I always had a conviction that failure becomes a failure only if one accepted it. I decided to be stubborn, and not accept it until it became inevitable. No more sentiments and I would face the adversities boldly. Strength out of the blue began to shield me. I knew that I was helplessly cornered, yet I was able to focus more sharply and became stronger, mentally.

I decided to the meet the examiners with a hope to convince them of my helplessness in the unexpected weather conditions. Who knows, everything might get sorted out if I was lucky enough. I did not look beyond that at that time.

Before stepping into the practical examination hall, I went to the washroom, cleaned my face, combed my hair, and put on my suit again. The suit was by then wet, shabby and full of wrinkles, and had lost its novelty.

This definitely was not the way I had dreamt for years to appear for this examination, which had meant everything for me. All dreams seemed to have perished in the rubbles of misfortune. I must be looking like a buffoon now, I thought and felt!

Damn!

The examination was conducted in three sessions, a short case session (within a stipulated time of, say 30 minutes the candidate has to examine as many patients as possible and organize themselves before the examiners for discussion), a long case session (only one patient is examined in detail) and finally the viva. It had always been mandatory that the candidate should attend all the three sessions, for its successful completion. The exam was programmed so as to finish all these sessions on the same day by all means. There would be six examiners altogether, two for each session, and all the candidates were arranged in three groups. At no point would a set of two examiners be repeated for a candidate, and thus a candidate would have to face all the six examiners by the time he or she went through the process. The examination, at any rate, would not be held in the same hospital where the candidate was attached and trained, and thus it became a genuine exercise and no factors other than a candidate's ability and potential influenced the results.

I followed the signboard that led to the examination hall, and saw a group of young people standing at the other end of the corridor. From the looks of their attire, I figured they were candidates who had either finished, or were still in the process of examination, waiting for their turn.

What about me?

I must have missed my turn already. I had lost all hope that I could join the group assigned to me. Even if they did permit me, all the other candidates in my assigned group would have finished the first session by now.

So what was the possibility that I could join them?

I had never heard of Royal College permitting a candidate who failed to report on time to be a part of the same exam later on. Even if some miracle did happen by chance and I was allowed to attend the exam, I could only take two sessions. A separate third session was certainly not going to happen, I asserted mentally.

I was not daring enough to let my mind think about how and when this miracle would happen.

I took a closer look at the candidates standing there, and found something different from the usual examination scene.

What was happening?

All of a sudden, like a fleeing fleet of alerted birds, hopes began to soar with a thousand wings!

The examination had not started yet!

Because of yesterday's heavy snowing, traffic had come to a standstill and some of the examiners from Edinburgh had not shown up yet. They would arrive soon, I was told!

I let out an audible sigh of relief, and I didn't care if anyone heard it or noticed. I felt like sipping ice-cold water in the scorching sun, and my body began to cool from top to bottom, giving me goose pimples. God had not ditched me into the filthy bin of destiny; instead, he had given me space to breathe again. I felt like an out of water fish falling into the deep water again, and my mind began to bloom with new hopes and dreams. Maybe other problems lay ahead, but at least I had something to hope for, at this point of time.

The exam started at 12:30 PM, after a delay of four and half hours. With the help of a registrar who was assisting the examiners, I borrowed a stethoscope and a few other things needed for the clinical examination. I did both the clinical sessions exemplarily well. A sense of wellbeing filled my mind.

CHAPTER ELEVEN

The miracle

It was 5:30 in the evening when all of us had finished the two sessions. There were only four examiners, as two had still not turned up because of the snowfall. So, inevitably, the last session of the examination, the viva, had to be postponed since the previous set of examiners could not be repeated.

Everyone was waiting outside for an official announcement. And at last the announcement came,

"All candidates are requested to attend the viva session at the Edinburgh Royal College Office tomorrow."

This did not surprise me, as I was anticipating this possibility when the examination was delayed. Yet it worried me. This decision of the college was not a problem for all the other candidates unlike me. My return ticket to India was booked for the day following the next day after the examination i.e., Wednesday early in the morning from London. To attend the viva examination I had to reach Edinburgh the following day i.e., Tuesday. But at what time the viva would finish I was not quite sure. It would be impossible to cover nearly 600 kilometers from there to Newcastle and subsequently to the London Heathrow Airport. Travelling such a long distance, that too depending on public transport, would be very risky and not to mention the strain involved. Moreover, I had already reconfirmed the ticket for Wednesday a week ago and I was not sure if it would be possible to defer it to another date. In case anything untold were to happen, buying a new ticket would be beyond my means. So far, all my expenditure had been precognited and hence each and every penny was valuable to me. There was nothing more in the account to meet unforeseen circumstances. Adding on, it would be difficult to contact the travel office so late in that evening.

I called up my friend in Newcastle and told him of my situation; he assured me that he would get in touch with the travel office and see if it was possible to postpone my travel to a later date after Wednesday. I set aside that problem for the time being and started looking for the lady registrar who was assisting the examiners. She helped me in procuring the necessary tools for my clinical examination and I felt at ease with her in addressing my concerns.

When I explained all my difficulties to her, she was very empathetic and listened to my story in all earnestness. She seemed to understand my difficulty, and in fact no one could be blamed for the current situation. The previous day's snowing had been the worst ever seen in the UK over the past few years.

I stood alone outside the exam hall. All the other candidates had left already after the announcement. I was still continuing to wait for the registrar who had given me a patient hearing. Was any sort of serious meeting going on between the examiners and the Royal College regarding my issue?

The viva session should not be a problem for most of the candidates. If at all one fails, it is usually for the clinical session which tests for more skills. In my case, I had done those difficult sessions remarkably well. No one can hide the body language which was sometimes spontaneous and natural, and I had seen my examiners act comfortable with me which had really boosted my confidence. I was able to do a good number of short cases correctly, and that might have placed me in a comfortable level, as far as the scoring of marks was concerned.

While my mind was grazing over the greenery of pleasance, I saw the lady registrar come out of the hall towards me.

Did her face look more hopeful?

Or was it my imagination since I was longing for a positive response?

As she conveyed the news, she seemed happier than me.

For a moment, I was unable to conceive what she said, I had started the morning witnessing a very bad omen, and according to traditional belief the entire day should have been spoiled. Yet God was now unrolling the red carpet of hope in front of me to march on. I do not know whether anyone had experienced this in their past.

To me, it was just something unimaginable.

I can only remember the British people with gratitude. Of course, there was this event when a lady British Consultant Doctor behaved inhumanly to me while I was attending her clinic. However, this type of social injustice was not a new experience for me. I had tasted its bitterness earlier while I was in Malaysia. It still sticks out like a sore thumb in my mind. But as for now, a miracle was on its way.

A separate viva session exclusively for me was to be conducted in the same evening!

This meant that, for the viva session, I would surely have to face one of the two sets of examiners, with whom I had already done the previous sessions.

In the examination system of the UK, the examiner did not know or count anything about the candidate's past, and the only thing that counted was his or her performance on-the-spot. They might not even know anything about the candidate's nationality, his skills, or where he was trained. In my case, by this time, they might have already inferred that I had come straight from India, probably with hardly any exposure to overseas training.

I felt a bit relaxed when I realized that I would have one more go with one of the previous set of examiners. In order to prevent me having an upper hand would they make it tough this time?

Though unnecessary, those concerns momentarily pulled down my enthusiasm.

Finally I finished the viva with the same two examiners who had tested my communication skills during the long case session. I had a difficult task of convincing them my skills and to add to that I had to tackle two issues at that time; first the temperament and adamant attitude of my patient's mom and second, her hard to digest Scottish accent.

The lady was very argumentative, and had some strong convictions regarding her child's illness, which did not agree with the current medical knowledge and practice. The examiners might have thought this to be a Himalayan task for me. However, by God's grace, I was able to convince her with my point of view in a way that was comfortable for both of us. The examiners had seemed to appreciate this as I could decipher from their faces.

The questions during the viva sessions were mainly related to the kind of treatments exclusive to high profile tertiary level hospitals. The logic behind such an attitude might be multifold. It could be to assess how well I would cope with a stressful situation, unlike the previous sessions which were a breeze. They had not known that I had worked in a reputed tertiary level teaching hospital in Malaysia. At the end as they concluded the session, I said with my palms together in the traditional Indian way of greeting, "Namaste!"

My eyes were filled with tears as I said it.

Did they notice it?

The tears had everything of an average Indian soul.

I noticed their faces. The message was clear; the happiest moment, for which I had been waiting all these years, was here at last!

Finally I saw the registrar, said the same 'Namaste' to her and noted down her email id.

I was ecstatic. As I stepped down the stairs of the examination hall I felt light and buoyant. My head, so far burdened with heaviness was finally free like a lightweight balloon.

CHAPTER TWELVE

Edinburgh Railway station, Scotland

It was 6:45 in the evening. Many roads were perilous and blocked, yet I had to hurry. I should reach Newcastle by the next afternoon, at any rate, and from there find a way to reach Heathrow on the same day Despite all of this my mind was still laid down by thoughts.

With hardly 35 hours left to reach London, I had already informed my friend not to postpone my ticket, due to the uncertainty of the examination.

Luckily, there was a bus to Edinburgh, the capital city of Scotland in the late evening from the Kirkcaldy bus station. The roads were covered with a heavy circle of snow making the travel difficult. The transport network had been hit badly with roads closed after accidents. Many trains were cancelled and airports were warned of severe disruptions, I was told. The bus took longer than usual. Somehow I reached the Edinburgh railway station at 8:45 PM.

I found out that services to many routes were cancelled at Edinburgh while others had been delayed for long. My train to Newcastle was cancelled as I had anticipated, and was expected to resume by early morning the next day.

I could not see the usual crowd in the station because of the unexpected turn of events. Outside, it was freezing cold. I had always been more intolerant to cold than heat. The sweater was not helping much.

How was I to spend the whole night in that railway station in this chilly weather?

I did not have enough money either to stay at a hotel or have a proper dinner. Luckily, I was told that I could use the same return ticket for the next morning travel.

There was a glass cabin on the platform.

I did not understand its purpose, but saw a few people smoking there. Actually, it was a shelter, but it had been closed at 10:00 PM. I felt very hungry, tired and sleepy. What would I do next? The chill was causing goose bumps and rigor all over my body. I was never used to this type of weather and winter in my life.

I saw a policeman sitting in front of something that looked like an outpost. I told him that I was an Indian doctor enroute to India after attending an important examination and was presently stranded there, looking for a comfortable place to sleep for the night, free of cost!

I said so in one sudden gasp.

I did not know what impression I might have gotten on him. He might have felt some sympathy, seeing my skinny structure and hearing my voice so low. The next instant, I found him contacting someone over the phone. He was in fact looking for a charity organization where I could be accommodated that night free of cost. After a few attempts, the policeman expressed his helplessness with regret. The temperature outside was dropping further, perhaps even below the zero degree Celsius mark. My fingers had turned numb and started to become blue and wrinkly at the tips. The station was almost empty by then. The big clock by the wall showed 1:25 PM. I was desperately looking for a bit of warmth. I started moving on the platform slowly, to keep myself warm. The cold wind was getting worse. Then I noticed the policeman beckoning me back.

Did he have something to offer me after all?

He mentioned about a rehabilitation center, which was hardly a 15-20 minutes' walk from the station. Advising me to approach them to find out whether they could offer help, he gave me the directions. I did not ask him for any details, like what the rehabilitation center was meant for, or what sorts of people were living there etc. Knowing such things were not my priority at that time.

I couldn't see any traffic in that direction, and the narrow icy road looked very lonely, except for the streetlights and some bushes on either side. It was a frightening experience, walking alone through an unfamiliar area that too so late in the night. As I had not had any food the whole day, I didn't take my anti-diabetic pills fearing the danger of hypoglycemia. The day had really been tiresome and exhausting, right from 5:30 in the morning. I had no choice, and started to walk with my carry bag, all alone in the way directed by the policeman. I did not understand his directions completely, as he was speaking too fast. I was not able to stick with his accent too. Now I wanted somebody to direct me properly to the rehabilitation center.

But how would I meet someone in that deserted street, that too, in the midnight?

I was all alone, accompanied only by my long shadow. I did not see anything else moving, except for a few rodents that looked like giant rats which crossed the road and vanishing into the deep bushes.

I had no idea if I was moving in the proper direction.

Then I saw a few shadows moving, quite far away at the other end of the road. I increased my speed, and they became clearer. The streetlight made them more visible. The silence was scary, only to be interrupted by the sound of my footsteps cracking the ice.

The shadows turned around.

Were they moving towards me?

Now I could tell the gender of the shadows.

I started feeling a little defensive.

My pace became slower and slower and breaths became faster.

Have the shadows stopped moving, or are they moving towards me?

Something seemed to glow intermittently, in that darkness.

What could be their intention?

In no way could I be a worthy prey to them, and I had nothing in my pocket but for a few pennies.

Now I was face to face with them. They wore skimpy dresses, and sexy-looking luxury black shoes. The mini shorts and body hugging tops were struggling to contain their lavish flesh in the front and back as well. I remembered the articles about the red-light districts in Mumbai and Calcutta.

I wondered how these young ladies spent time in the darkness, waiting for their customers.

They were not advancing further, as I had feared. I smiled at them, and said in a calm, low voice,

"I am an Indian doctor looking for the rehabilitation center which is somewhere around here."

Maybe my skinny body, complexion and destitute look gave them the picture of a poor Asian Fakir!

Did I annoy them as I would not be worth a penny for them?

The cigarettes were glowing intermittently, like burning pieces of charcoal. Both of them were talking to each other, loosely holding the cigarette between their red lips. The cigarette kept dangling up and down with their lip movements.

They had ignored my existence altogether, I thought. There was no eye contact, or any other sort of communication. Taking deep puffs, both of them started to blow off dense smoke rings by the subtle movements of their tongues.

Suddenly, like a reflex, one of them threw the cigarette into the bush and signaled me to follow her. That sudden and unexpected response startled me for a second. Neither of them had uttered a word to me till then. The communication remained quite nonverbal. I followed her a few yards to a crosscut road on the left, which looked like a runway at the airport. At the end of it in the thin, scanty light, I could see the rehabilitation center building.

The strange company I had in the dark had not troubled me in any way and on the other hand, they had given me invaluable help at that odd hour.

I said 'Namaste' again, but that did not evoke any response from the woman. Her face remained blank, leaving me in doubt if my simple gesture of gratitude was understood at all. I thanked them mentally, and slowly proceeded to the center through the dark.

CHAPTER THIRTEEN

A new dawn

There was a small light in front of the main doorway of the single-storied building. It was already past midnight, and the front door was shut. Surely everyone would be asleep by now. Even then I could hear people talking inside and I pressed the calling bell switch just once. After a few seconds, a middle aged gentleman opened the door with a pleasant smile.

I told him the purpose of my visit and he welcomed me warmly. I saw a few people of different ages sitting around a big table in the main hall along with a few young ladies and teenage boys. Their scrimpy clothes exposed dark green tattoos on many parts of their body.

The body piercing with silver studs and metal hoops in their earlobes, lips and belly buttons were particularly striking. Seeing me at that odd hour, they might have thought of me as a new member of a different race.

Anyway, the comfortable shelter in that center was a great relief indeed from the freezing cold outside.

The middle aged gentleman introduced himself as the chief of the care staff and professional counselor of the center. He was in charge of the residents. He thought that being a doctor, I would be interested to know how the center functioned and hence volunteered to give me a short brief.

Drug addiction had emerged as a problem of great public concern in the UK. People, especially youngsters had begun to involve in addictions ranging from heroin, crack, cocaine, alcohol and gambling. Many of them indulged in this to evade the grinding realities of life and subsequently ending up like the moth flying into the candle. The very idea of these sorts of rehabilitation centers was to guide these unfortunate deviants of the society to the mainstream like a herding dog.

While enjoying the hot coffee he offered, which helped me warm up a little. I was very much receptive to him. The wrinkles and the bluish tinge of my fingertips had started to disappear.

He took me to a small room which was cluttered endlessly like a junk room, with dust laden empty boxes, old books, broken furniture, step ladder, dismantled electrical appliances and so on. But I couldn't find a cot, bed or a pillow. He expressed his helplessness to offer something better for me. In fact I didn't need any such 'luxury' rather I simply needed an 'even surface' to lie down and some warmth. He handed me some thick cardboard covers and newspapers and my bed was ready! Two thick telephone directories served as a pillow.

I felt like I was at the bottom of the deep blue ocean but barring the angry roar of the waves or even the fibrillations. Dead silence prevailed everywhere. During that deep sleep, my mind was blanketed with a mysterious bliss, waiting for a new dawn on the horizon! I never ever had such a sleep with an absolute peace of mind, at any point of my life.

The man woke me up early in the morning. My train to Newcastle was at 6:00 AM. He gave me a nice sweater to wear, hugged me and with a handshake wished the best for my future! I thanked him in my traditional style. The sun had already started to set. The landscape was getting dimmer and dimmer; like a huge glowing ball of orange and yellow filling the blue canvas of the sky, the sun descended with its radiance leaving behind a magnificent display.

The train was moving very fast, and the whimpering of my mind was lost in the loud grinding of the wheels. Everyone and everything marched past backwards, leaving behind an ebullient sense of nostalgia . . .

****

Exactly three weeks after my safe return to India, I received a letter from the Royal College of Pediatrics and Child Health, London. The content of the letter was the fruitful end of the passionate scribbling I had done on a piece of paper, years ago!